RECLAIMING WHOLENESS

Letting Your Light Shine Even If You're Scared To Be Seen

BY KIMBERLIE CHENOWETH

COPYRIGHT

Difference Press, Washington DC

Copyright © Kimberlie Chenoweth, 2015

All rights reserved. No part of this book may be reproduced in any form without permission in writing from the author. Reviewers may quote brief passages in reviews.

ISBN: 978-1-942646-97-6

Library of Congress Control #: 2015958153

DISCLAIMER

No part of this publication may be reproduced or transmitted in any form or by any means, mechanical or electronic, including photocopying or recording, or by any information storage and retrieval system, or transmitted by email without permission in writing from the author.

Neither the author nor the publisher assumes any responsibility for errors, omissions, or contrary interpretations of the subject matter herein. Any perceived slight of any individual or organization is purely unintentional.

The memories shared in this book are from the author's perspective and should in no way be construed as representing any one else's perspectives. In order to maintain their anonymity in some instances identifying characteristics and details such as names, physical properties, occupations and places of residence may have been changed.

The information in this book does not constitute medical or other professional advice and should not be used as a substitute for the medical care and advice of your psychotherapist, physician, or other health care provider. All decisions about your individual treatment and care should be made in consultation with a qualified psychotherapist or other health care provider. The author is not responsible for any adverse effects or consequences resulting from the application of any of the advice, practices, or procedures described herein.

Cover Design: John Matthews

Editing: Kate Makled & Grace Kerina

Author's photo courtesy of Kelley Cox

PRAISE FOR
RECLAIMING WHOLENESS

"Kimberlie Chenoweth's book, *Reclaiming Wholeness*, eloquently, authentically, and courageously chronicles her rich, life-rendering journey into wholeness. With rare unwavering trust, Kimberlie bravely and unconditionally encounters great challenges and gradually welcomes them all — darkness, doubts, vulnerabilities, fears, love, longings. She acquaints herself with, holds, honors, and, yes, cherishes all she harvests from within and from the outside world. Her voyage transforms her to a state of wholeness — the modern 'Ithaca'. The reader will be self-inspired and with Kimberlie's wisdom at hand, readily able to enhance his or her own life's journey. And I'm sure, you the reader will be hungry for more, as I am. This is an author we need to keep hearing from as she continues to explore the human journey beyond known horizons."

PETER TSANTILIS, PH. D. | Clinical Psychologist, Mentor, Lecturer

"In *Reclaiming Wholeness*, Kimberlie Chenoweth demonstrates her own connectedness with our mother earth's vital energies by transmitting the teaching directly through her words. With profound honesty and enthusiasm, she will guide you towards your own wholeness — 'an organizing principle of consciousness.' A master in a long spiritual lineage, Kimberlie practices that orientation as a place to come from in each moment. I highly recommend this wonderfully real, energetic, and warmly encouraging book!"

ANNE HILLMAN | Author of *Awakening the Energies of Love: Discovering Fire for the Second Time* and *The Dancing Animal Woman: A Celebration of Life*

"*Reclaiming Wholeness* is a companion volume for anyone interested and daring enough to be the authentic author of their life. With a kindness that seeps from the pages into your heart, Kimberlie will take you on a life-affirming journey from the perils and joys of childhood, through a dynamic process of personal healing, and ultimately into a palpable experience of belonging to something much greater than just yourself. *Reclaiming Wholeness* is about coming home."

ALEXANDER LASZLO, PH. D. | Director of the Doctoral Program in Leadership and Systemic Innovation at the Buenos Aires Institute of Technology in Argentina | 57th President and Chair of the Board of Trustees of the International Society for the Systems Sciences | Co-author with Ervin Laszlo of *Mind Beyond SpaceTime: The Continuity of Consciousness in the Cosmos* (forthcoming)

"As I began reading Kimberlie Chenoweth's little book, Reclaiming Wholeness, I repeatedly found myself saying aloud, "Yes, yes!" If you're a seeker like me, you're bound to love how Kimberlie describes not only her work in helping people rediscover their roots, their connection to our earth, but also her own experiences, often painful, which gradually led her to her calling. She draws you, the reader, in as a friend, and writes you sweet personal letters addressed as 'Dear Seeker.' If you've been shut down by childhood trauma, or if you don't feel as though you belong and aren't sure of your purpose, Reclaiming Wholeness will not only comfort and assure you, but give you concrete ideas and a definite plan for how to reconnect to your authentic, indigenous life. Even if you've been on religious or spiritual paths that have eventually disappointed you, this book offers ideas that will ground you, open your heart to your own value, and lead you home. *Reclaiming Wholeness* offers a compelling way to discover and grow your authentic presence as an emergent expression of the divine here on earth."

AMY DUNCAN | Composer, Arranger, Pianist | Author of *Getting Down to Brass Tacks: My Adventures In The World Of Jazz, Rio, And Beyond*

"*Reclaiming Wholeness* guides us down a cathartic path of self-healing and personal redemption. Kimberlie Chenoweth delivers a powerful narrative with style and heart. Brava!"

EVAN MICHAEL ZISLIS | Author of *ClutterFree Revolution: Simplify Your Stuff, Organize Your Life & Save the World* | Founder of Intentional Solutions

"*Reclaiming Wholeness* is deep and soulful, a true journey into an authentic way of being in the world."

CAROL PETERS | President, Peters Management Syndicate Inc (talent management)

DEDICATION

*For all the light seekers
ready to shine here
on earth.*

FOREWORD

The heart of mentoring lies in stewarding one's mentees into wholeness, a dynamic state of creativity, well-being, and fulfillment. If ever there was a great example of this process — the momentum of teaching and initiation giving rise to new expressions and dimensions of wisdom in action, this book is it. As Kimberlie Chenoweth's long-time mentor, I have seen her do the deep dive she stewards her own mentees through, and I've seen her emerge time and again victorious — in every aspect of her life and the conscious ways she lives it.

In these pages you will find only truth spoken — for there is no other language spoken in the deep dive of our healing — and you will find that the great truth most needed in modern life is, in fact, the very core of this story. This truth is: in order to thrive we need to *be in the process of healing*, and that healing process can only be engaged through a long arc of well-guided experiential work. Healing work for humans is a layered process that requires sacred time and space to unfold; it cannot be achieved in a 'weekend wonder event' filled with someone else's lofty thoughts. It is in many ways a process not bound by time — it simply requires our direct engagement in order to learn about, and from, ourselves, over and over again, one deep dive after another. It requires tremendous courage and the willingness to live in the moment, even as we re-experience our past. It is a process that, by its nature, saves us from isolation and carries us back into the very things we seek — our identity securely held and dynamically supported in full collective consciousness. And since full consciousness includes all of life and the vibrant land we live on, in the process of our healing we are also rooted into our collective membership in life and an abundant collective relationship with the whole living planet.

Kimberlie sets this stage, pulls back the curtains, and using her own story, invites everyone to participate. This is an invitation into a new kind of membership, and by accepting, we stride together into collectivity, a courageous step that needs to be taken in our world in spite of current social and cultural resistance to collective dimensions of consciousness and relationship.

Kimberlie's understanding that 'wholeness is a verb' — i.e. it's action-based — reflects the power and momentum of her own unwavering healing journey, and it has led to the development of her most important themes. First, she states that everything we need to find our healed state and regain our longed-for wholeness comes from the same place: our connection to the land. To make a connection we have to *take an action*. Secondly, she reminds us that the 'how to' for rekindling this connection resides within indigenous wisdom. This is wisdom we need to *actively reclaim*. This leads the reader to a third theme, which is our need for a practical connection to 'Spirit' as it has been understood in the great wisdom traditions of indigenous cultures. I'm not speaking of contemplative traditions, but of the extraordinary cultures that preceded the contemplative movements, cultures whose consciousness functioned at such a high level that their innovative powers and achievements sound like science fiction to most modern people.

For indigenous people *power*, *medicine*, and *knowledge* are the same, and they are all aspects of 'Spirit' — of the invisible forces and intelligence out of which our visible world constantly emerges. For indigenous people, connecting to Spirit is a *required action taken for practical personal and culture-wide benefit*. It is the action of 'going to the source' and allowing not just one individual but entire cultures to be 'fed' and 'informed' by the very powers and universal intelligence that have always fueled long arcs of well-being and conscious evolution for humankind, at least until modern times. To call on the powers of the land, and Spirit, and the universe at this high level requires full collective consciousness in action. Yet in the modern world, where we've come to value individuation so highly, a call to act 'collectively' can feel threatening to the ego's solo idea of itself. This means, as Kimberlie so wisely advises us, that we must re-craft our identity in terms of membership and belonging to the generative powers of the land. We must know ourselves in terms of our original capacity to 'source' those powers in order to craft thriving realities for everyone.

In full consciousness, we benefit from the attributes of allowing the land to speak us into being: we live in membership, we wear our healed state every day, and we direct our awareness outward, into the world, to discover energies, ideas, and visions that we can grow to their highest states of fulfillment. In full consciousness this kind of 'living into thriving' is done collectively — everyone has value and that value has a role to play; everyone is supported in growing and using their value; no one is left behind; and the wisdom gained through creating states of thriving and wholeness is retained and passed on generation to generation. This is how humans used to live, and their wisdom is still available to all of us. It is the experiential record of our species, and frankly, we can't afford to lose it.

In emphasizing the importance of indigenous wisdom, Kimberlie reveals the greatest secret hidden in plain sight — that within this data base of human experiential wisdom [what we call indigenous wisdom] there resides a set of organizing principles that can generate the wellbeing, peace, and prosperity we so desperately seek in our troubled world. The only 'catch' is that we can't strategize or think our way there, meaning the ego can't map the route, nor can the 'I' within us drive us there. Instead, we have to be actively seeking our healed states as members of a greater evolving whole. We have to take the deep dive to recapture our true human identities as members in life, and in doing so rediscover our collective natures, for only in collective consciousness can we access the genius we have for thriving in wholeness.

The principle of wholeness is a key component of this body of wisdom, and rest assured any who trust their process to Kimberlie's mentoring skill will learn these timeless principles that organize human awareness for thriving. To reclaim the kind of consciousness that gives us access to these principles, it is critical that we remember ourselves as a collective species, designed to thrive together, not apart. It is critical that we stop compartmentalizing, separating, and owning, disowning, or otherwise controlling everything around us — all actions that are inherent to untended states of emotional wounding.

What Kimberlie is offering is a clear and fierce pathway into full presence, belonging, support, and freedom to craft a thriving reality. She is offering the reclamation of wholeness. Wholeness is achieved in part by changing how we use awareness. It is achieved by using awareness to know our world through relationship, not by disconnecting in order to defend. It is achieved by using awareness to discover potential and use it to create abundance, not by tolerating the inevitable scarcity of isolation. Solo or collective, isolated or linked, loose like tumbleweed or fully rooted in our gifts — these are the choices, and they seem obvious in a list of words, but this is a challenging path that we must take together, not alone. This is the function of the 'elder' in society — to be the guide for those who are coming along the path behind us. They are the ones who will be carrying our legacy forward, and it is as important for them to know the value of being mentored as it is for those ahead to be the skilled and patient mentors.

In telling her story, Kimberlie clearly states the value of the mentor and illuminates the beauty of the mentor-mentee relationship. She replaces a hierarchy-based view of mentorship with the power of experience and loving presence. She puts fear in its place — as a power to source, not to run from. And she unfolds a critical insight into this thing we call relationship: without clear relationship with ourselves in membership with the land and with our communities, there is no wholeness. This is the hidden rainbow bridge in Kimberlie's work — that the long arc of an authentic healing process is *simultaneously* our bridge into full collective being — the only kind of 'being' that consistently produces states of thriving and fulfillment, where we are fully connected with one another and supporting one another in wholeness. In fact, I think Kimberlie makes it quite clear that this is the only kind of 'being' we are truly designed for.

Kimberlie's story will touch your heart and challenge your soul. I hold the vision that her story will also help you understand that the exquisite power of the human spirit — *your* spirit's power to reach out, heal, connect in love, and create abundance — deserves to be rekindled now. And if it happens within enough of us, it will happen in the world. This is the magic of reclaiming our wholeness, and we shouldn't waste a moment thinking about it. We should just dive in.

Thank you, Kimberlie, for this beautiful and courageous gift.

Marti Spiegelman | Founder, *Shaman's Light™: Indigenous initiation and mentoring for your genius; Awakening Value™: Technologies of Consciousness for Thriving in Business*

TABLE OF CONTENTS

- 1   INTRODUCTION
- 4   CHAPTER ONE   **Belonging and Becoming**
- 12   CHAPTER TWO   **Childhood Memoir**
- 36   CHAPTER THREE   **Finding a Way**
- 54   CHAPTER FOUR   **Seed Tending**
- 66   CHAPTER FIVE   **Original Wholeness**
- 81   GROWING FORWARD
- 85   ACKNOWLEDGEMENTS
- 89   ABOUT THE AUTHOR

INTRODUCTION

Who am I? Why am I here? Where do I belong?

Dear Seeker,

The source of our existential questioning is not what you might think.

As I walk this earthly walk, crossing paths with friends, clients, family, I hear some version of these questions nearly everyday. "What's my work in the world?" "How can I be fully 'me' and part of a community at the same time?" "Where's my tribe?"

They're my questions, too.

Time feels of the essence, as we haphazardly try to balance the urgency to find voice, right work, and a place for passionate purpose with the everyday chop wood/carry water aspects of our lives.

Our choices are seemingly unlimited, yet this illusion of infinite choice is itself a burden for many.

And the world becomes crazier and more chaotic every day, so at times we feel hopelessly adrift with no promise of a safe landing.

Add to this the effects of childhood wounding through which many of us learned to (or were forced to) shut down our authentic expression in the world.

For some it really does seem as though there is no hope for their own dreams to be realized, much less for humanity itself to survive these precarious times. How do we become "not lost," in order that we might eventually be found in our right places?

But we do know we're here for a reason — to help others, to steward the earth, to play some part in the massive awakening on the planet.

We're the ones who identify as the healers, shamans, artists, light workers, perhaps the highly sensitive, inspirers and even leaders of others. And yes, most of us faced our fair share of adversity growing up. So we do yoga, meditate, seek out spiritually like-minded people, walk labyrinths, long for time in nature, and hire coaches to help us find our niches. We travel to (or want to travel to) Peru, Ireland, northern Alaska, or Nepal.

But it always feels like something's missing, right?

There's something big inside longing for expression as we yearn to reveal our true nature and purpose, and then to discover where our presence will make the most difference in a fast-changing world. If you can relate, this book is for you.

But where do these questions come from? Why are they so prevalent in today's world? I believe their source is two-fold.

We've lost our roots in the land.

And

We've been forced into an inner world much smaller than the actual world we were designed for.

I want to share with you what I've come to know about an original experience of wholeness that's ever present, ever available and reliable.

Wholeness. A state of being so connected to earth and Spirit that we inherently have everything we need — to know who we are and where we belong — and to create a life of flourishing.

Shall we dive in?

Looking forward to the journey with you,

With love,

Kimberlie

CHAPTER ONE

Belonging and Becoming

"When we became accomplished in our manipulation of the material world, we forgot the underlying spirit of things, the original source from which all came into being. Now we suffer because we sense something missing, but we do not know what it is."

GLENN APARICIO PARRY, *ORIGINAL THINKING: A RADICAL REVISIONING OF TIME, HUMANITY, AND NATURE*

Let me ask you this: Do you live where you were born?

Most likely not. Most of us have picked up and moved at least a few times in our lives. We're a transient people, cut off at the roots with each transplanting into a new locale. So how are we to know where we best fit in? We want to experience meaningful belonging, but we're living a myth of separation and disconnection from the land, from each other, and from our own hearts. It's the rare person who experiences him- or herself as one with the earth. Walking on pavement so much of the time, we don't really feel the ground beneath our feet. In this daily disconnection we have forgotten what it is to live in reciprocity with the land that feeds us. At its worst this forgetfulness manifests as the clear-cutting of forests, the dumping of plastic waste into our oceans, and the pillaging of the earth for oil and gas.

Contrast this with the mountain villages of Peru, where I've traveled and trekked a number of times. There, the people mostly live where they were born. They know who they are. They know they belong in and to their families, their communities, their villages, and — perhaps most importantly — the land. For countless generations, their families have stewarded the land, and they continue to actively create relationships with the fertile soil and towering mountains and pristine waters around them.

These heart-centered people look like they're literally rising up out of the earth — emerging like beautiful flowers or the colorful crops of corn and amaranth growing in the fields. The earth feeds them, and they feed the earth, in a relationship of beautiful reciprocity. They identify with the land and water, with the mountains rising around them. They *are* the land. And they don't struggle fretfully with questions of identity and belonging the way you and I do. (Caveat: This is becoming less true, as the young people are increasingly enticed away by dreams of modern life in the cities, but that's a subject for another time.)

During a recent visit to the mountain region of Ausangate, I was sitting in circle with other students at 12,000 feet with massive peaks rising about us, and Don Francisco Apaza — one of the *paqos* (shamans) who works with our group — said, "I am a child of one of these mountains." He meant it literally. "Thanks to this mountain, I can lead and teach others in the way of the wisdom I've been gifted." Francisco is a powerful expression of Apu Ausangate, an emergent confluence of the energies of that mountain, knowing exactly where and how he belongs. He and others of these indigenous villages walk in deep resonance with the land, with Pachamama, our Mother Earth.

Francisco's mentor, Don Manuel Quispe (the late, beloved elder and spiritual leader of the Q'ero nation in the Andes), taught that, "Our belonging is to the earth and the mountains, the rivers and the forests, the winds and the clouds. We come from the belly of the earth and return to the stars, and until we understand this, we will not have the power to evolve."

I go to Peru to work with indigenous healers and teachers, to learn and experience the timeless wisdom of wholeness that they teach. They show us a way of life that supports both authentic individuality and genuine belonging. And I am convinced that the time for remembering (literally, re-membering) ourselves as children of the earth is now, now, *now!*

But transiency is only part of the problem.

Our disconnect from the land has created a multi-generational culture that does not fully honor the needs of children. Through time, Western civilization came to value the thinking mind over nature's wisdom, and to see children as extensions of their parents, rather than as the unique expressions of nature they truly are. The challenges of a disconnected childhood, or childhood as raised by disconnected people, can take such a toll on our psyches and souls that we grow up not entirely sure of who we are or our places in the world. So, of course, we tend to play small, so others may not notice our uncertainties. We want to look good in the eyes of others, but it's at the risk of our own authenticity. We certainly don't want to risk rejection!

Whether the messages of our caregivers came at us overtly or covertly, we grew to believe that we weren't enough. Or we were too much. Or both! We learned that our wants and needs weren't as important as our parents'. That it wasn't safe to express our feelings. We learned to shapeshift, crafting our responses to optimize the chances of getting some semblance of acceptance, love, and recognition from them. But in order to manage that adaptation, we had to bury aspects of our authentic selves for which there was no room. We had to disappear important parts of ourselves! Perhaps this pattern has persisted into our adult relationships and social behavior.

For many of us, early experiences of trauma, neglect, or abuse blasted our young hearts and minds out of our bodies and into some other world of our own making. For me (and I'll be sharing more of my story in the next chapters), early challenges sent me both inward and upward — out of body, out of feeling, and into the great big world of Spirit. Others escaped to the wilds of the forest or creek just down the road, or into music, art, or some other safe venue. Nearly all of us developed overly active thinking minds that helped us figure out exactly what our next move should be, according to the written or unwritten rules of the situation.

These escapes had great survival value, but they also left us handicapped in other areas of our lives.

So we ended up as walking wounded, having sustained blows to our individuality and identities, as well as to our sense of belonging.

How many people do you know who are still trying to figure out what they want to be "when they grow up?" Perhaps when they are in early adulthood, or at midlife? Even on entering a traditional "retirement" age? People who don't really believe they have something of value to bring to the world? Who are forever searching for their place of belonging?

And how many others have given up on the question, or perhaps never even thought to ask it?

I'm writing for the people who haven't given up, who are still asking some version of these important questions.

Even if you've found some placing or landing for yourself, do you still wonder if maybe you could be, should be, want to be doing something *more*?

I know there's a big longing inside you, alive and well, and I know you have big dreams! Are they unfolding as you want them to? Are you giving them room to grow?

Are you even still hiding parts of yourself? Your magic, your genius, your unique purpose and passion for being here at this amazing time on planet Earth? It's a question that works as well reversed — are parts of yourself still hiding *from you*? Does it seem you can never quite get to the core of who you are? Or that the central thing that's dreaming in you rises in your soul long enough to remind you, *"Hey, I'm still here!"* only to get lost again in... you name it. The daily grind... not knowing what steps to take next... old beliefs about your value or capacity... or even lack of support for bringing all of you forward into the creation of *your* meaningful work in the world?

But I also know there's big strength inside you, good protoplasm that helped you get here, right where you are now. There's something inside you that preserved the dream (and *you*) — so you could one day, finally, find yourself and land the work you are meant to do. A client said to me last week, "I know there's big power inside me, but it gets tweaked around my throat and I can't get it out." Another carries a marked polarity between feminine and masculine energies inside herself, requiring tremendous courage to weave them into a coherent whole that doesn't value one aspect of her beautiful being over the other. And yet another was so tapped into her origins in the stars, it took massive courage to find ground under her feet so she could shine in *this* world!

And so, in addition to the possibility of learning how to connect with earth in a whole new way, we have a need to heal whatever keeps us from shining our light fully.

I believe we have been given an amazing opportunity to clear all that gets in the way of discovering, embodying, and living as our true selves — in alignment with our biggest dreams, where they'll make a difference for others.

And through the clearing, we get to reclaim our original innocence, power, and love.

I've by no means got this all figured out. I came in challenged from the beginning, and learned the art of invisibility and "hiding" my self and my gifts early on. But I also came in with a good deal of determination and persistence, and something at the core of me that always knew I was here for a reason. I refused to give up. I found different paths, and collected insights along the way. I looked for and found core principles to guide my process. And I've been lucky enough to have teachers and mentors with whom I continue this lifelong journey of healing, all while exploring what it really means "to come from the land."

So, hand in hand, these two important dynamics go — healing and reconnecting with earth — reweaving each of us into the tapestry of life and of the land. Through sharing my own story, I hope to offer some novel perspectives on healing the effects of a challenging childhood. They're not new, but they're also not talked about so much.

I hope that through making some of my own process visible, you'll gain some ideas for your own journey of healing and whole-ing. I hope you'll garner at least a few gems that help you reclaim what's rightfully yours — your true nature, your potential, and your place in the world — in indigenous wholeness.

Dear Seeker,

This is your heart speaking. I'm holding a vision for your life, for the full manifestation of your potential in the world.

I'm the nudge you feel to follow your dreams, and I want your wholehearted *attention! Are you listening?*

Are you saying the biggest "YES!" you possibly can to the magic I see in you? What's holding you back?

Let's muster all the love we can to open the way for you... so you can rock your beauty and brilliance the way you're meant to!

In wholeness,

Your Heart

CHAPTER TWO

Childhood Memoir

"If you bring forth what is within you, what you bring forth will save you. If you do not bring forth what is within you, what you do not bring forth will destroy you."

JESUS, GOSPEL ACCORDING TO THOMAS

Dear Spirit,

You know what you put into me. You know where and why you originally spoke me into this world. You know what I'm here to do, and you knew it would take me half a lifetime to home in on it. You've fed me the beauty of amazing landscapes on several continents, and you know the challenges I faced as a child.

You've brought me through so many challenging scenarios and dynamics, taught me more than I ever could have dreamed possible! Yet there are stories, secrets, really, that I haven't been ready to share with others beyond my closest allies.

Until now, Spirit. You've delivered me to this moment with a big nudge to start writing. Not because my story is unique, but because it is not.

Please be with me as I write, and with my readers as they read. Let all that I share be in service of healing and wholeness.

You have my heart,

Kimberlie

It's a bit strange to write about your family of origin when your parents are still alive, especially when you (well, I) have been committed to downplaying or hiding, to disappearing as a means of coping in this world. My previous training as a psychotherapist also discouraged this level of personal sharing, so this is the first time I've shared much of my story publicly, and I'm feeling a bit shy and reluctant as I begin to write. But the need for truth-telling trumps the need to hide, and the telling is ultimately about the triumphs — the gifts, joys, and wholeness available to any of us who take on a journey of healing.

I'll be describing some painful events that set the stage for my two-fold process of healing and finding my place in the world. I hope to explain my own disappearance in a way that sets a context for the return journey to wholeness as I've come to know it. In turn, I hope you'll recognize and understand more of your own journey, whether you are just starting or well along the way.

Many of my clients, when they start talking about their childhoods, are hesitant to get into their stories because "My parents did the best they could," or, "I can't blame them." Or they'll say something like, "Other kids had it a lot worse than I did." To which I respond with "Your experience was your experience. In many ways, this isn't about your parents. It's about facing the reality of your experience. And it certainly isn't about comparing what happened to you with what happened to someone else. No matter what happened, it affected you the way it affected you, and that's what we're here for. We're here to help you heal."

I want to emphasize that I have deep respect and appreciation for what each of my parents had to endure in their early lives. Through my own healing, I've found a place of deep understanding of the losses and traumas that shaped them as kids, too. Since these things tend to be multi-generational, I'm sure they could each recount similar stories of the difficulties they faced.

Plus, they both brought something vital to the unfolding of my spiritual lineage — seeds of spirit from each lineage planted in my bones without which I wouldn't be who I am or doing the work I do. I'm the latest, and, with no biological children of my own, the last representative of those lineages as they've unfolded in me. I don't take this lightly. While I've always felt that I was here for some important reason, to do some profound work in this world, perhaps, it's clear that my legacy will be carried forward by people not of direct biological descent. I hold this reality close to heart.

That said, it's also important to note that every challenge encountered and faced has made me who I am today.

Everything I share with you is from my own perspective, based on the ways that I, a sensitive little girl, perceived and experienced what happened. That doesn't mean my experience is the way anyone else in my family experienced things. While my sisters remember me as being a good, but bossy big sister, I remember retreating into a world of my own making, with very little interaction. Doesn't mean I wasn't there, it just means my experience — my way of dealing with reality — placed me into a different perspective. So be it. All views are true.

....

Montana. The word is magic in my mouth. Even as a kid I'd proudly proclaim, "I was born in Great Falls, Montana." It was special, and it made me feel special, particularly since I grew up mostly in New Mexico, and even though we left Great Falls when I was two months old and Montana when I was two and a half years old. I had no idea what "Great Falls" would reveal to me until decades later, but the Montana part... well, that's always meant *home*.

On a cold winter morning in mid-January, in a hospital along the shores of the Missouri River in Great Falls, Montana, my mother was about to give birth to the first of her five daughters.

The story goes that the doctor checked her out, concluded it would be awhile, and left her on a gurney in the hallway with her mom, my grandmother. But I defied him. I was ready — eager, even — to get here, in part (or so my spirit says) because I knew I was here for a reason! And my grandmother recognized all the signs of my imminent arrival, called the doctor back — *stat*. I came through quickly and, I like to think, jubilantly, anticipating a hero's welcome.

I'm waxing imaginative here, but bear with me, because I believe every newborn has the right to be fully, lovingly, authentically welcomed. And what happened next posed the first conundrums of my life.

First, according to my dad's sharing of the story years later, when he saw the wrinkled little newborn me, he exclaimed, "I don't know what it is, but I made it, I'll live with it." He thought it funny, having never seen a newborn before. And perhaps it was funny in the fuller context of those times when a dad's introduction to his child was looking through a plate glass window at the little bundle swaddled in her bassinet along with other new arrivals. Even though I know he felt pride then and always for his family, I think some part of me felt the "it" aspect of what he said and registered a core question: Was my true nature going to be honored here?

The other conundrum? I was given a name that didn't fit. My mom told me, years later, when I changed my name to Kimberlie that she should have listened to her instincts and named me Kimberlie, as she'd wanted to, because she knew that's who I was. Instead, they came up with Barbara Kim, in deference to someone in the family who didn't care for the name Kimberlie. So, I grew up with a first name that not only didn't fit, it actually means, "foreign, a stranger." Which certainly didn't help my tendency to feel like a stranger in a strange land! Years later, an awesome mentor asked me, "Are you going to live the rest of your life with a name you don't like?" I immediately replied, "*No*," and owned Kimberlie — "of the royal forest (or fortress) meadow."

We left Great Falls for Columbia Falls when I was two months old, and then moved on to New Mexico when I was two and a half years old, my mom very pregnant with my next sister. Dad was going to work in the Anaconda Mining Company's office in Anaconda, New Mexico, out in the desert between Grants and Gallup. Anaconda was a uranium mining community built for the white company guys who hired local Native Americans to go into what we now know were radioactive mines.

Years later, my husband and I revisited Anaconda, which by then had been abandoned. It was an eerie ghost town, but the sites were familiar, and I found both the houses we'd lived in. On another trip a few years later, it was all gone. The land has been "reclaimed," with only a few cottonwood trees marking the spot where once was a lively little community. How strange to find a significant placeholder of my history disappeared from existence.

My family lived in Anaconda for three or four years. While we were there, I loved to be outdoors, catching and stroking horny toads' soft underbellies, or making mud pies, which consisted of rolling Velveeta cheese in the brown dirt of our neighbors yard. I so wanted them to taste good, a blend of decadent creamy orange pablum and earth! My mouth still waters for the highly anticipated bliss of my creation, but of course they were inedible.

My best friend, Vicki, was a year older than I was. I loved to go to her house because her mom let us move the furniture around, spreading blankets between chairs to build wonderful places of imaginative play and escape. Going to Vicki's was always a fun adventure!

One day, Vicki talked me into visiting the community hospital and clinic. I'd never been in a medical building before. I was enthralled and thrilled to be out on such an adventure. Problem was, I was just three or four years old and our parents didn't know where we were. So, while we were peering through the door into a room where an old, old man lay shriveled up in a hospital bed, a friendly nurse asked our names and called our parents.

My mom, of course, was thoroughly worried and not the least bit happy with me. It was a long drive, that short distance from the medical center to our house. She'd made waffles for dinner. I got to eat, but in a deafening silence, and then I was sent to my room. And so I learned early on that obedience was going to be key to my well-being in this family.

Perhaps even more informative to my early roots, we were living in the New Mexico desert, and it is Native land. That desert earth, home to very recently indigenous people now living on nearby reservations, got into my bones, as did a more indigenous way of being that I've spent a lifetime trying to liberate. Living on that amazing land, I tucked away deep inside something of my authentic *earth beingness*, in kinship with a way of life that's deeply of the earth.

In fact, I had a dream one night after a visit to one of the pueblos, when I was four or five years old. In the dream, my room was a kiva, with a beautiful ladder leading down into the sacred underground chamber. It was a secret room — no one else knew it was there. My sanctuary. And so I learned early on to withdraw to a safe place within myself as life became increasingly challenging.

I have lots of respect for that child. A strong one she was. Sweet, and always a bit of a mystic, with an occasional flare of the tempest. One of my earliest memories is of standing on the window side of a closed curtain, enthralled by the thunder and lightning storm gathering in the desert.

Before Innocence Lost

In the time before innocence lost, I rode the rocking horse bareback and free under the New Mexico sun. Horny toads befriended me, their velvety soft underbellies delighting my young, unworked hands.

In the time before innocence lost, a Father-Mother God sang to me of love as I embraced the high-fidelity maker of music that played for me my favorite song.

In the time before innocence lost, earth was home. Mudpies and adobe fed and sheltered me, or so I dreamed. The ladder led down to my room, private kiva deep in Pachamama's womb.

In the time before innocence lost, I stood on Acoma's mesa, stronghold of desert silence, ancestral ways — sensing red in my white, freckled skin.

In the time before innocence lost, I stood gazing out the window, curtain closed behind me, brave heart quickened by the storm gathering on the horizon. Lightning and thunder.

A thousand one. A thousand two. A thousand three...

....

We moved from Anaconda to Albuquerque as I started kindergarten. By that time, I had three little sisters and another on the way. Albuquerque is where my core childhood wounding begins, centered around the death of my youngest sister and its profound impact on me and my family.

But first, you should know that both of my parents were raised in the Christian Science religion, and we went to church every Sunday. Well, I went to Sunday School, and there we grew up with a different kind of God than most people do. God wasn't a bearded guy up above who looked out for and/or judged his children. God was a verb. God was Love. God was Spirit, Soul, Mind, Principle, Life, and Truth.

God was both Father and Mother. And this is this foundation on which my experience of spirituality was formed.

Christian Science is also known for its radical reliance on God for healing. Founded by the visionary Mary Baker Eddy in the late nineteenth century, she claimed to have discovered the "key to the scriptures," the secrets of Jesus' healing abilities. Rather than rely on medical diagnosis and treatment, Christian Scientists turn to prayer in times of need, prayer that insists if we are made in the image and likeness of God, then we are spiritual, not material. Healing is possible through denying the existence of disease, and claiming our perfection as children of God.

My first (and I think only) experience of physical healing through Christian Science came when I was four or five years old. I'd been sick, and one afternoon found I couldn't move my legs. This was before the polio vaccination became available, so it's possible (but, of course, unconfirmed) that this was the onset of paralytic polio. I do know my legs were paralyzed, and my mom was scared. She called a Christian Science practitioner, who said prayers and gave what's known in Christian Science as a "treatment," as described above. I remember lying on my parents' bed as she made the call. My mom then lifted me into the bathtub — and sat beside me as I soaked. I remember the quality of my mom's presence, her concern and her love, her desire to do the right thing for me. The problem resolved within a few hours.

I have wondered if the paralysis was a manifestation of me feeling crippled by a lack of the support I desperately needed — but needed not nearly as badly (I'm sure I concluded) as my younger sisters (one who came in colicky and the other two rambunctious twins). In that moment, however, my needs superseded theirs, and my mom was there for me.

Then along came Kathy Jo, my youngest sister. My mother had to have been overwhelmed. I was already getting lost in the mayhem before Kathy was born, dedicating myself to being good, obedient, and mostly staying out of the way. I learned to turn away from my naturally curious, authentic self in order to try to figure out what my parents needed from me, and then give it to them. I disappeared into the background.

But I had a moment in the spotlight when Kathy was born. I got to the hospital with my dad to bring her and my mom home! It was enough of a treat just to get to tag along, but then I got to hold her — alone — in the back seat all the way home! I'll never forget how happy and special I felt being such a big girl holding my new baby sister. I couldn't wait to show her off to my other sisters and grandma, waiting at home.

That proud moment didn't last long, though, not even to the front door of our house. Before I could get out of the car, Kathy was lifted from my arms so my mom could, of course, carry her inside. In my childlike mind I somehow believed I would be the one to carry her proudly in, no doubt anticipating that the feeling of being special would last. There's a revealing photo of my mom holding Kathy, turning to face the camera as she's about to enter our front door, and me looking at the camera, too, confused and confounded.

I became more lost than ever in this family of five little girls born within six years of each other.

My response? I redoubled my efforts to be as obedient and helpful as I could be. Usually that meant just staying out from underfoot, but as I got older I also took on helping around the house. It was important to me to try and make things easier for my mom.

When I was eight, and Kathy almost three, she got sick. Real sick. My grandmother, mom's mother, flew in from Montana to help out, and again a Christian Science practitioner was called for prayerful treatment. No medical treatment was sought.

As I remember the course of events that winter, Kathy worsened and fell into a coma, with a brief rally one day when that rosy little face of hers with slightly chaffed, red cheeks, came to life. She sat up on the kitchen counter, very thirsty, demanding glass after glass of grape juice from our mom.

I have no idea how long she stayed awake (a few hours?), but she did fall still again. Her crib was replaced with a big double bed, where I think she and Grandma slept. I remember sitting in a chair beside the bed and reading to Kathy from the Christian Science book of healing, hopeful of another rebound, planting some of the first seeds of my desire to be a healer.

On Christmas Day, Kathy lay unaware on the couch in the den, as a fire blazed in the fireplace. Our Christmas tree stood all lit up in the corner beside the fire, gifts under the tree and up on the mantle. My gift for Kathy was on the mantle. I'd wrapped it all by myself and very especially for her, using colorful ribbon to proudly and painstakingly create a "K" on the front of the package. She never got to open it.

A few weeks later, just before my ninth birthday, Mom and Grandma came in to my room to waken my sister and me and tell us Kathy had passed on. They explained a little about what that meant, that she was living in heaven now, something along those lines, and they gave us the option to stay home from school that day if we wanted.

I was torn, but decided to go to school, where I wanted to let my teacher and classmates know what had happened. When I got there, another girl in my class let us know her mother had just died. And so I said nothing, because, really... isn't it worse to lose your mother than your sister? I imagined her pain, and swallowed my own, creating a mask of okayness as I went even more deeply into hiding.

As a family, we were unable to process the death other than with occasional references to Kathy herself. She had died of complications from spinal meningitis.

I must say, I can't imagine my mother's grief and the life-long journey of healing she has had to face. Such a huge mix of emotions haunting her, right alongside the demand that she continue to show up as best she could for the rest of us. After Kathy's death, she disappeared inside a poignant private hell — struggling with deep grief and depression — even as she did her best to outwardly carry on with mothering and with her own life.

Shortly thereafter, I woke up with the flu one night, nauseous, dizzy, and scared. I can only imagine now what must have been going through my little mind. Do I go get my parents? Will they take care of me? Am I going to die, too? Huge questions for such a young girl!

Way too sick to handle this alone, I woozily felt my way down the forever long hallway to my parents closed door, hesitated before opening it, and entered their dark room.

Most of my memories from the next few years disappeared into a haze of fear, grief, and isolation, of believing my pain to be somehow less worthy of attention than others' needs, and watching helplessly as my mother withdrew.

But I do remember something that happened when I was in fourth grade. I had a big, painful, angry boil on my chest. I was deeply embarrassed about this, and so I endured it silently and alone at school, until a classmate inadvertently hit it like a bullseye while we were learning the Hawaiian hula dance. Choking back tears, I ran to the coat closet at the back of the room, embarrassed to show my pain. A little girl came to check on me, and then the teacher — and of course I downplayed the event, feeling both ashamed and *way too visible*!

Speaking of visibility, this may be a good place to weave in another formative experience — an example of how two people can have vastly different experiences of the same event. I couldn't tell you for sure how old I was, probably ten or eleven, and I had no conscious memory at all of this until my dad reminded me many years later, even though it affected me profoundly.

By now you might guess that it was rare for me to say or do something that might cross either of my parents, but apparently on this particular day, I did.

My dad was not pleased with me, and clearly intended to spank me.

Until that day, the two red wooden paddles hanging in a conspicuous place in our house were more than enough to discourage any misbehavior from me. One was a big fraternity paddle, and the other a smaller sorority paddle from my parents' college days. If you were going to get in trouble in our house, you always hoped it would be the smaller one in the big person's hand.

I have no recollection of whether either paddle was ever used or if they were just there as threats to encourage good behavior, but I'm certain neither of them was in my dad's hand on this day of reckoning for whatever I did that angered him. And I was not about to be spanked by any means, so I ran from him. He gave chase, catching me by the arm. I looked back and up at him from a forward bending body still in motion away from him —

and my dad, so startled by the apparent terror in my eyes, let me go.

For his compassion, I'm grateful, but the interaction cut deep without actual blows. From then on, I lived with an added layer of fear, along with a new, intensifying sense of anger that could not be safely expressed.

I began to have sleep disturbances, and to be unable to fall asleep at night. I'd lie in bed, silently longing for my mother to come comfort me, but afraid to call out to her. The silent longing became a silent cry. Eventually, it became a silent scream when our garage was remodeled to be an additional bedroom, giving me my own room but on the opposite side of the house from the rest of the family.

How many nights did I crawl into bed, listening for sounds of the intruder I was sure lurked outside my window? For how long each night did I hold myself completely still, afraid any movement would provoke an attack? For how many years did I bury that scream of terror, so certain that to scream would bring death? This progression of fear is a great example of how unexpressed feelings take up residence inside us, grow in stature and power, and ultimately take on lives of their own.

Following years of consciously holding back that scream, I eventually sent it underground, only to have it re-emerge in a really frightening way. For many years after I left home, I endured "night terrors." I would frequently wake up to the sound of my own piercing scream shortly after falling asleep at night — some ghastly intruder about to off me in my dreams. Some nights I'd wake up halfway across the room, and once I actually tried to escape through a brick wall. Ouch.

If you've ever experienced anything like this, you know it is terrifying — for the dreamer and for anyone else in the house! Through the years, a few clients have shared similar stories.

While it may be easy to pathologize the phenomenon of night terrors, I prefer the take of one of my mentors: "It's your power coming back to reclaim you."

Think about that! Imagine the power it takes for a child to hold back emotions they know their parents cannot or will not tolerate. I'm ever in awe of this capacity. Author and psychologist Alice Miller calls it "The Drama of the Gifted Child" — the child who is bright enough, sensitive enough, emotionally aware enough — and apparently powerful enough — to completely shut down emotions she knows aren't welcome here.

It's worth mentioning here a discovery I'll talk more about later: that the power it took to send unwanted experience underground is still available to us — to you — ultimately to be reclaimed through a healing process that will free you to stand visibly in your power, rather than using it to hide.

For now though, back to the child me. By fifth grade, the soft, innocent, alive eyes so evident in my first-day-of-first-grade photo had given way to a clear absence of life in my school photo. I was gone, my essence and life-force stuffed so far inward it no longer shone out of my eyes.

But then… *grace*. Something in me started slowly waking back up. It might be called longing. Longing to be seen and to connect. Longing to rediscover the parts of myself that went missing. A longing to be whole.

The comeback started later in fifth grade, with some indirect bids for attention. I cried out for help the best way I knew — at school — first with forged notes excusing me from the rigors of PE, and later with a triangled bandana holding an uninjured arm close to my chest as I swigged from a bottle of vanilla I hoped look like medicine.

Medicine? It was a foreign word in our house. Remember, we were the people who "didn't believe in doctors." Medicine was something other people took to make them better. In our house, we relied on prayer, as was expected of Christian Scientists. We were the ones who didn't smoke or drink alcohol (except sometimes in secret like my parents sometimes did). We were good. And we relied on God to heal us.

But I badly needed some kind of medicine, or healing perhaps, and I didn't know how to say it outright or even to express my needs at all. My teacher noticed. She sent me to talk with the school counselor. That's where some of my anger began to pour out. "I'm in fifth grade. I don't want my mother to wash my hair anymore. I should get more than 25 cents a week for an allowance."

It was a beginning. I opened up as best I could to someone who was willing to ask the right questions and then let me talk. Better yet, someone who actually listened and took action, too. I got a raise, and I got to wash my own hair. With the right information, my parents were able and willing to respond.

I also discovered tetherball. The only sport for which I had any affinity at all also gave me a place to release some anger. I was good. I discovered I had a competitive streak, and I hated to lose. But I loved the feeling of my hand connecting with that single volleyball-like ball tethered by rope to a pole, my single-minded mission to smack it all the way around, bypassing my opponent's opposite swing, until the ball reached the apex with a satisfying bounce back as it reached the end of the rope. My first taste of success. More importantly, a taste of belonging. I was good at something. My life had more meaning when I played (and won) tetherball.

I also had an extreme ability for competitive memorization. Even in Sunday school, with the books of the Bible. I had the names of the books of the Bible all memorized by the time I was about seven. Later, that skill served me well in getting decent grades. I was bright, but too bound up emotionally to really learn well (not that the educational system supported my experiential learning style). At any rate, my ability to memorize what I needed to know for the next day's test helped me get through grade school, junior high, and then high school with minimal effort on my part.

It wasn't until later, in high school and college, that I connected with a couple of teachers who began helping me bring my own voice to the conversation through writing, which grew to be an important and loved outlet for me. One of the first essays I ever wrote, as a high school senior, was about removing the masks we wear to hide our true selves from the everyday world. It was another hint about the work that lay ahead for me: helping others to remove their masks and reveal their true face — authentic and pure.

Between starting junior high and graduating high school, we moved from Albuquerque to Arlington, Texas, then to upstate New York, and ultimately on to California's San Fernando Valley. With each move, I grew a little bolder. Inherently shy, I typically walked the halls of high school with eyes cast toward the floor.

Then I decided to do something that felt really bold and brave: look people in the eye and smile. And, instant reward, they smiled back! I joined the pep squad. I started going to the boys' swim meets because my boyfriend was on the team, and ended up co-managing the team with a girl who became a dear friend. Then I joined the girls' swim team... just for the fun of it, because I certainly wasn't a strong swimmer!

I also joined a church youth group, enjoying fun outings and doing some community outreach with them (visiting elderly church members, creating holiday meal baskets for people who could afford them, helping with cleanup after a huge flood–that kind of thing.) Somewhere along the line,

I was pegged as a leader within the group — a reality that still surprises me. What did they see in me? It'd be easy to chalk up the honor to the possibility that I'd fooled them, but the reality is that being in leadership roles felt strangely right. Looking back now, I think others saw a strength that I couldn't yet acknowledge. I took on those roles with gusto, but I never really felt fully embodied in them. I just knew to smile and pretend I knew what I was doing.

Spirit always seemed to prepare the way for me.

By the time I got to college, the darkness inside was wreaking havoc with my inner life, but outwardly all looked good. I chose Principia College in Elsah, Illinois, a liberal arts school and the only one in the world specifically for Christian Scientists.

I had friends. I got to move from the dorms to live with the family of the Dean of the College, where I stayed for nearly three years. I was elected to a leadership position in the on-campus church.

I tapped more deeply into the metaphysics of Christian Science, in part because it made sense to me and brought me joy. But also, I truly felt like I belonged in and to the world of Spirit, not this world. It was a world of absolute Love and Truth, and as long as I could stay in that high place, I was fine.

But that world sat right next to a world of rage and fear that occasionally roared up inside me. Not outwardly, mind you.

I would never have revealed so much to the outside world. Inside me... yeah, at times it was so active I thought I would explode. The two worlds were in polarity, both bursting with energies so big I didn't know if I could hold them. I liked the first a whole lot more, but that didn't keep the other from rising inside, so I learned to bear it, to smile my way through the nasty waves of negativity when caught in that undertow.

Years later — lucky to find leading-edge approaches to inner healing — I discovered that those storms could also give me access to the most creative, core expressions of my authentic self. More on that in the next chapter.

As part of my undergraduate program, I spent ten weeks traveling in Norway with a group of students and our sociology professor, studying the educational system there. I don't remember much of what I learned about that topic, but I do remember the land.

Mountains and fjords, stunning landscapes. Farmland. People deeply connected to the earth through generations of land stewards before them. I was deeply impressed by the sense of history as I stood inside a 1000-year-old church in Oslo, struck by the contrast between that and the comparatively nascent history of Anglo-Saxons in the United States.

But I especially remember walking the land north of the Arctic Circle, where my own indigenous soul rose up and took notice of the wide expanses of tundra inhabited by the indigenous Sami peoples, to which I was sure I belonged.

Walking alone one day, beyond the local town we were visiting, I wished I could just keep going forever through those expansive landscapes. For the first time ever, I felt like I'd come home. Claimed by the land.

The next summer, I went on another adventure offered through my amazing liberal arts college: backpacking through the Wind River Range of the Rocky Mountains. Two weeks prep in Colorado, then four weeks in the wilds of Wyoming. Mind you, I was nowhere near physically ready for a trip of that magnitude, but my heart and soul knew it was vital for unfolding the DNA of my authentic self. Traversing that high land with a small group of students, our Austrian professor, and his wife, I began to see my capacity for showing up — even (especially?) when facing extreme conditions. High winds, rain, broken tent poles, feet raw with blisters. There were days I was certain I could not take another step and then I did it, over and over again. It never occurred to me to complain or give up.

That capacity, to do whatever it takes to get where I want to go, had been forged in childhood and it served me well in the Wind Rivers, but it would be decades before full appreciation took hold.

I found another piece of my soul in those mountains, and then I graduated to life in the "real world."

Dear Seeker,

The reason I'm sharing my story with you is in hopes that you'll recognize something of your own story. We're so good at downplaying and disappearing that we can walk right past the gems buried in the struggles. I hope my story helps you start connecting the dots so you can bring your real dreams to life.

Even if it isn't yet clear to you how, I want you to know that there are clear hints given in the pathways you've traversed that can help you unlock the secrets of who you are and the work you are destined to do.

I also want you to know you're not alone! If you're like me, you've mastered the art of figuring things out for yourself and forging ahead solo... because isn't that what we've always had to do? Well, despite having that great skill, I believe that we benefit most when we find someone to guide us into and through the most challenging aspects of our wounding. Without that witnessing and guidance, our greatest gifts can go unrevealed.

So, just bear this in mind as you read on. I'll be sharing some aspects of healing with you that aren't widely known or talked about and that can make all the difference to you making the difference you long to make.

With love,

Kimberlie

CHAPTER THREE

Finding a Way

"The feeling of longing, one of the most important feelings in the organism, reflects its need for contact with its environment and the world. Through belonging the soul escapes the narrow limitation of the self, without losing the sense of self or being that is our individual existence."

ALEXANDER LOWEN, M.D., *BIOENERGETICS: THE REVOLUTIONARY THERAPY THAT USES THE LANGUAGE OF THE BODY TO HEAL THE PROBLEMS OF THE MIND*

Fast-forward a few years, to me in my mid-twenties and moving to Colorado with friends. I'd been accepted to travel abroad with the Peace Corps, but I had a longing to put down some roots before taking on more global travel. Looking back, I can see how my future work continued taking shape with that very conscious decision to "put down roots."

Shortly after landing in Colorado in 1982, doubts that had plagued my experience with Christian Science grew to the point I had to face them. With courage (and it did take courage to come clean to those who were still strong in the religion), I "closed the books" on that chapter of my life and began a new search, actively seeking Truth wherever it might appear. I read Alan Watts, Ken Wilber, and

Carlos Castaneda. I discovered the mystical Persian poets, Rumi and Hafiz. And I fell in love with the poetry of David Whyte, whose work inspired me to be true to my essential nature and has served as an important guide on my path of authentic becoming.

I also discovered psychotherapy, having landed a front-of-fice position at the local mental health clinic. I started reading the self-help books and therapeutic books on the shelves of the clinicians, learning a lot about both healthy and unhealthy parenting. I started therapy for myself, with someone who specialized in codependence and adult children of alcoholics. I even started a local Adult Children of Alcoholics group.

Eventually, I married a man who has lived nearly his entire life within two miles of the place he was born. Seriously, I committed to putting down roots! We live on several acres of land in Western Colorado, with gorgeous views to the south and west, and with an immense expanse of red sandstone rising up behind the house.

It was during the early part of our relationship that I began facing the challenges of my childhood, with their inevitable effects on our marriage. I came into the relationship with no idea of the degree to which I was still in hiding. As I began healing and waking up, the assumptions we each held about marriage were challenged. So were our interactions with each other, often! As our conversations became increasingly courageous, each of us was compelled to grow in ways we would not have done otherwise. It's the subject of another book entirely, but I will say that "marriage" has certainly become more verb than noun, more a committed process of relating than a thing in and of itself. As I now believe it should be!

In 1990, I earned my master's degree in counseling and started a private practice, even though I never identified with the idea of being a psychotherapist. I was clear about wanting to work in some healing capacity — and, with a career as a Christian Science practitioner off the table, counseling was a means to further that dream, a way to keep alive my desire to heal and be healed.

Along the way, I discovered a beautiful healing process called "Core Transformation," developed by Connirae Andreas. Core Transformation set an early template for the deep emotional and spiritual healing to come. Very simply put, the template is: *Start with whatever thought, feeling, or behavior you want to change. Let yourself have the experience of it, no matter how painful or distasteful. Love and accept the part of yourself creating the unwanted experience. Then start asking what that part of you really wants, at deeper and ever deeper levels. Eventually, you reach a stream of energy at the core (Love, Spirit, Beingness, Oneness, Okayness) through which the original unwanted experience is transformed.*

I loved Core Transformation so much that for a long time it was central to my work with clients. I went on to become a Core Transformation trainer and I still occasionally offer Core Transformation workshops. And so another piece of my own becoming and belonging began to unfold: that of teacher and trainer.

And, then, in the mid-1990s, I found a source of the kind of reliable, universal, go-to wisdom I'd been seeking seemingly forever. Or, more accurately, it found me. An ancient, mystical, land-inclusive spirituality out of the Andes found me three times, through three independent sources, even though I couldn't even have known to look for it!

This is how Spirit works, right? By placing us right where we need to be to get what we need to get. There's no way any of us could ever be forgotten or left behind. We're more completely looked after and loved than we might imagine, beautifully tracked by the very thing our hearts most want and need. Or so it has been for me, and I believe it's possible for you, too, if you're not already experiencing this. There's so much magic going on "out there" — more than we know, more even than we possibly could know!

It started in 1995, when some colleagues brought a Peruvian shaman to the Utah desert. He had been raised in the Andes, near the Andean nation of Q'eros. (The Q'eros are a living lineage of pre-Incan people who escaped to the mountains at the time of the Spanish conquest.) I was spellbound by his love-presence. He was a mystic who taught poetically; a seamless stream of spirit and earth wisdom that I immediately recognized as both universal and highly personal. I thought, "*Yes.* This is how the world works." That weaving of spirit and earth rocked my world with a strong sense that

I had found my spiritual home.

At that point in my life, I was again experiencing the night terrors that had plagued me as a young adult, and I wanted to ask the shaman for his take on it. With the help of our translator, I explained what was happening and requested his input. His response was simple and direct: "You must enter through a different door." I had no idea what he meant, but my insides jumped up and down and said, "Yeah. Truth."

Later that day, we headed toward a boulder-strewn canyon for some solo meditation work. While most folks hiked alongside the canyon, I climbed straight up the middle of it. The shaman followed me. Stalked me like a jaguar hiding in the forest, as those hiking above later told me. I don't recall the full instructions for the meditation itself, but I really *wanted* to have a big experience. I struggled. I tried. I failed. And finally, toward the very end of the allotted time, I gave up. As I released all expectation and simply let myself be, an ethereal puma came right up to me, opened its mouth, and roared — engulfing my face in light. Okay, cool!

Heading back down the canyon, I shared the experience with our translator who replied, "That's entering through a different door!" Returning to our desert campsite, I had the chance to share the experience with the shaman, too. His response? Identical: "That's entering through a different door."

The shaman also, at one point, said, "*El trabajo consiste en volverse luz,*" which means, "The work consists of becoming light." *Yes,* that resonated deeply. Even though I was having profound experiences of earth during those wilderness workshops, I still thought returning to light somehow meant transcending corporeality. Light and land, energy and form were still separate processes. (I now understand this very differently, as you'll see in the next chapter.)

Here was someone speaking my language, and I wanted more. I loved the poetic way this man spoke. I loved being seen. I felt truth at the core of what he taught, and I wanted more. He promised to introduce me to mystics in Ireland and Italy and to work with me in Peru. I could be his *nagual* (apprentice), and I hungered for it all.

At one point, as the rest of the group sat in silent meditation with nature, I walked. No, "walked" is not the right word. I stood barefoot on earth. Paying exquisite attention to what happened between foot and earth, I slowly lifted one foot, and then slowly placed it slightly ahead of the other. A whole new stream of energy and information began to reveal itself in the relationship between earth and foot, foot and earth. There is, in fact, a whole universe revealed between the two...revealing itself to me still.

This earthy mysticism woke me at bone level.

The land is alive!

We belong to earth, to *Pachamama* — living, loving being, mother of us all.

I had begun to discover my own roots in earth, rising through the land to inform my presence on earth.

That shaman from Peru was not to be my ongoing teacher, however, and I cut ties with him after what I experienced as a betrayal of my trust. Still hiding, I didn't talk with him about it, but simply moved on, until I became ready to deal with it later in other ways.

Then, in 1999, I learned about an event that was to take place, also in the desert, offered by another well-known teacher of Andean shamanism. A Peruvian elder would be the guest of honor for a week of teachings, ritual, and explorations on beautiful Navajo land. The Peruvian elder, Don Manuel Quispe, was the spiritual and political leader of the Q'ero nation, a man with whom my first teacher had grown up. (Don Manuel has since made his transition.) Don Manuel's presence was palpable, even with 90 people participating in the event and little opportunity for direct interaction! Solid and clear, full of unconditional love and acceptance, his presence radiated through the canyon and into our hearts.

Excited to be back in the field of the *oh so intriguing and inspiring* Q'ero tradition, I decided to register for ongoing training and initiation with the sponsor of that event, the first segment of which began a few weeks later. Overall, the program wasn't a great fit, though, in part because of the large group size, and I didn't continue. (I did get clear that I had no interest in working with large groups — either as a student or as a teacher!)

Right around that time, in the mid-1990s, I started receiving visionary craniosacral sessions. At first, it was to relieve physical symptoms that had been accumulating through my life. All the emotion that I'd been holding back had to express somewhere, and it manifested in a number of physical ways. The energetic approach to this level of relief and healing was helpful.

At the time, the craniosacral work seemed magical. Profound. Transformative. This was bodywork at the energetic level for emotional, physical, and spiritual healing, and it got my attention, big time. The shifts I experienced were new and wonderful as I tapped a new ability to relax and release, to receive the work at a really deep level. As the work progressed, I kept going back because through it I was beginning to remember who I really am. My true identity was beginning to wake up, and wow did that feel good!

(Of course, I did fall asleep again, back into the old territory of fear and pain, anger and grief. And I woke up again. Again and again and again, as is the way of awakening. Don't let anyone tell you it's a one-time deal! Those folks who wake up all at once are rare, and even they still have work to do.)

I grew increasingly curious about this magical experience I was having and how it was happening, and started asking questions of my craniosacral practitioner. As my questions grew deeper and more frequent, he commented that he heard me asking for mentoring, not just insight. He gave me the names of three women who mentor healers and visionaries. One of them lit up brightly in my mind's eye: Marti Spiegelman. I went home, called her, and began training with her a couple of weeks later.

As it turns out, Marti had also been taught by Don Manuel, so this was the third time the Q'ero tradition found me. And this time it was a great fit! Two weeks after our first call, I was sitting in Marti's training room in Northern California with a few other serious students, learning about the Andean cosmology of presence, love, and light, and beginning to tap into Marti's vast expertise in how consciousness works.

Hungry, I took every opportunity to study with Marti through her Shaman's Light™ Training Program, saying *yes* to each level of training as it became available to me and continuing today with advanced training and research.

I've also made numerous trips to Peru with Marti, to research and receive initiation directly with Q'ero and other Andean masters. All of which is beyond the pale of what I ever dreamed might come my way.

It's primarily through Marti and our teachers in Peru that I've also discovered a whole new understanding of wholeness. Beyond a state of being we long to attain, wholeness is an organizing principle of consciousness, around which we can organize thought and activity in ways that bring us fully present (and visible), aware of our purpose, and flourishing as we grow our good work in the world.

It starts with the land. Don Manuel Quispe said, as transmitted by Marti, "When you understand you come from the belly of Pachamama and return to her when you die, then you'll be gifted power." And he didn't mean power over anyone or anything. He meant creative power.

Wholeness starts with a great big taproot into the land. A beautifully poetic way of saying this, a core teaching of the Andean lineages, is that "the land speaks us into being." Indigenous peoples have always known the land is alive and conscious, that human presence emerges through the land, and that the connection can't actually be cut (except by lack of awareness of it). Western culture lost touch with this reality when we began shifting awareness from *being* to *thinking*. We began exploring and valuing the world of thinking over pure, wide-awake experiencing. We diminished our connection to nature and got lost in thoughts, figuring things out, and spinning endless theories to explain the way things are.

But the connection can be restored, and we're being called now to re-weave ourselves back into the consciousness of the land. As we do so, we will once again call earth "Pachamama," our one true mother. We'll know ourselves as her children, informed by the land around us, but also by the landforms of our birth, where the universe originally spoke us onto the planet.

Our ultimate source is Spirit, but when we leave Pachamama out of the picture, we lose touch with vital aspects of wholeness — of our identity, purpose, and potential.

I'll be talking a lot more about wholeness coming up in the rest of the book, but first... this story wouldn't be complete without also delving more deeply into the importance of healing whatever stands in the way of rediscovering our individual, indigenous natures.

From our first meeting nearly fifteen years ago, Marti saw through the smiling facade that had brought me to her doorstep. She saw all the way through to the core of my authentic self — and helped me find my way back to it. It's a good thing, too, because in my work as a psychotherapist, I was already being called to help others rediscover their true nature, too.

Indeed, this is a great example of cultural anthropologist Angeles Arrien's teaching that "Where you're challenged is where you're gifted." Hiding behind a false face? I'll bet you'd be good at helping others find their true face!

I've come to expect that wherever I've been most challenged in my life, I'm likely to discover important pieces of my own work in the world. And I'm absolutely certain the same is true for you. "Where you're challenged is where you're gifted." What a great reason to go on the treasure hunt that the journey of personal healing offers!

Having seen through my facade early on in my work with her, Marti made a most amazing referral for me. As the first (and possibly only) person ever to see straight through the false face I typically wore, she held a truer vision of my potential. And she knew a deep-healing process would be required to free that potential. A proponent of Wilhelm Reich's discoveries about wounding, armoring, and the releasing of armoring into states of flow, and out of which the field of Bioenergetics emerged, she suggested I call a man named Peter for help, to clear the way for my natural, authentic self to shine through.

Peter, an extraordinary visionary, healer, and psychologist, has championed every fierce move I've made to claim my life for real. Born and raised in Greece, he is deeply informed by the lineage of that land. He knows his way around the profound depths of the human psyche. Through his presence and love, I've learned to be fearless (even when I'm scared) diving into the dank, dark underworld. By now, I know each dive will always bring an expansive emergence into even greater light. Beyond healer, Peter has become a true mentor, revealing the art of profound healing which I'm now bringing to my own clients.

Here's some of what I've learned: I know we're designed for love to flow freely through our hearts and out into the world. I know we contract when we can't express our feelings, and those feelings don't just go away. They get stuck, frozen behind layers of armoring designed to protect us until we get to a point in our lives where we decide to finally face what's in there.

While holding back feelings may have saved our lives as children, it can seriously mess with realizing our dreams as adults. We don't really know who we are when we've spent a lifetime shapeshifting. Eventually, to be free, we have to dive in and feel what's there, one layer at a time. Each dive releases a wave of expansive energy that feels really good, and then we work to sustain that expansion, diving in again whenever we come to the limits of our ability to sustain it.

At first, it is scary, but over time I've found that I actually welcome each new dive because I know the burst of life force that comes barreling through on the other side of it. This is how we retrieve our real power, the gifts we came to share with others.

Humans have been engaging the wisdom of the dive for tens of thousands of years. Just look at the myths of the goddesses Persephone and Inanna, both of whom entered the underworld in order to free something of value, and to find light in the darkness. Western culture tends to take a more cognitive, behavioral, and insight-oriented approach to personal healing, and while there's a place for that approach, it will never be enough for the kind of release that delivers us into the light of our own souls, where we have healthy access to the full range of human emotion, where our essential selves can blossom and flourish.

Releasing armoring can be like a mountain rainstorm letting loose on a hot, dry day in July after months with no rain. It releases a wave of good feeling that clears the air and resets our systems. If it's a really good, soaking storm, the grasses green up, flowers perk up, and earth herself gives a big sigh of relief as she receives that all-important moisture.

Releasing armoring can also be like puncturing or releasing a dam on a river. Designed to hold back the natural flow of water, the dam-release brings an initial burst of energy that temporarily upsets the old, forced equilibrium, and then eventually restores the rightful, life-sustaining flow of the river along its true course.

I happen to know about dams. I masterfully built them inside myself as I grew up, but they're also reflected in the landscape in which I was born. In Great Falls, Montana, there are five waterfalls within ten miles along the Missouri River. Originally, there was an immense conversation between flow and drop, flow and release, flow and wild abandon. Then several dams were built to generate electricity. A couple of years ago, I wrote the following short piece about my relationship with those falls.

Well, I'll Be Dammed

Your life force is like the flow of the Missouri River meandering through dark canyons and across the Montana prairie. The riverbed is well-defined by rock and soil as you find your way east. The journey is pleasant, a nice flow toward your destination, ultimately joining the Mississippi.

Passing through Great Falls, the terrain shifts. You come upon a waterfall, and the bottom drops out from beneath you. Your energy scatters, falls, submerges. You think you might drown.

You could die!

Yet there's something unusually thrilling about the fall. Something in you wants to dive, to go for it all and take in every titillating detail as you splash your way down to the next level. You hit the surface below, but you don't stop. The momentum takes you deeper, sinking into unknown depths where energies freed in the fall re-shape and settle, and it's here you might really die.

Well, something does die, and is reborn. You re-enter the flow re-formed. Then it happens again. And again. Over four more waterfalls you go. Five times in total.

Until your soul knows this cycle of freeflow, freefall, re-formation intimately. The journey informs everything you know about wounding and healing, about life in its natural state of flow.

And then they built the dams, which changed everything. Great walls of concrete erected from bank to bank to stop the flow and force it, compressed, through a manmade form to generate electricity. Man-made energy. They contorted your natural shape and authentic movements for their benefit. So you learned about being held back, slowed down, compressed, and reshaped for someone else's benefit. For electricity — a good thing, right? So you learned not to complain, and to sacrifice yourself at the place of once-sacred falling waters.

But the knowledge of your original flow is still and always there.

And dams can be dismantled. Though the flow will never be the same as it once was, it can be restored. — in your life, if not in the river itself.

You can heal, one dam thing at a time.

....

Speaking of dams, in the 1930s, my great-grandfather was instrumental in the contentious damming of a sacred waterfall on Native American land. The Native people had already fallen victim to the Homestead Act (which my dad's family had taken advantage of), having their lands reduced and their traditional ways of living curtailed.

The waterfall had been a place where offerings were made and sacred rites performed, but the white people's government maneuvered a way for a large dam to be built. There's a photo revered by my family, taken the day the dam's completion was celebrated. (I've never liked it.) In the picture, my great-grandfather is seen with a great big smile on his face, proudly shaking the hand of one of the Native chiefs — completely oblivious to the look of disdain on the chief's face.

I spent some time at the river below this dam several years ago, around the time I began exploring the role of dams in my life (both literally and metaphorically). An offering was created and prayers made in service of reparations for the role my family had played in the injustices done to the original inhabitants of that land.

We have much work to do, don't we? — to heal the wounds that bind us and to reclaim our natural belonging to the land.

I hope you're beginning to sense that, taken together, this interrelated process of personal healing and weaving ourselves back into the land can create an experience of wholeness that's been missing in the modern world, and from which we can each create the life of our dreams.

In the next two chapters, I'll unfold a bit more what I've learned about the process of healing, and then share more about the relationship between wholeness and the land.

....

Dear Seeker,

Good news! As Rumi says, "What you're seeking is seeking you!"

Your true essence is seeking you. Your authentic being longs for reconnection with you. She waits for you just the other side of this gateway you've arrived at, hands outstretched inviting you home.

If you do what you can do to claim your full presence as the person of vision and power you know yourself to be, you will discover your original indigenous spirit. You will germinate the seeds of your becoming and come home to the You who has always been there, holding the light for you and lovingly showing the way home.

You may well need mentors and guides along the way — people who can help you find your way to your true self. You don't have to go it alone.

There are way-showers in the world, people who have chosen a profound path of healing and are now here to witness, guide, and champion your potential as you move forward. I'm here to say that working with someone who knows both the darkness and the light of the territory you may need to traverse is invaluable.

With big love,

Kimberlie

CHAPTER FOUR

Seed Tending

"Every seed has a promise. If you plant it and take care of it, it will grow and show you what it is."

6 YEAR OLD ELISE

Since each one of us came in with coding that's unique compared to anyone else's on the planet, truly making a difference means doing what no one else in the world can do but you. More and more of us are discovering we won't be satisfied with anything short of realizing our unique, innate gifts. We're also discovering that to make the fully soul-satisfying difference we long to make may require a commitment to healing, to freeing ourselves from the results of childhood wounding that keep our authentic selves in check.

The reality is that much of our innate magic has been stuck in time, buried beneath layers of adaptive behaviors designed to please our parents and other important people in our lives. If you want to make the difference you're here to make, then it's likely you've been called to do some healing, too — to free up your authentic, unique gifts, and to support the full expression of those gifts in ways that resonate with your soul's deepest sense of purpose

It is hugely important that we claim the right to live free of the holds of the past — to rally again and again on behalf of what our Andean teachers call "your healed state" — to "wear your healed state everyday." Because most of us simply can't sustain a high level of self-realization without at least occasionally having to clear some muck.

Committing to healing doesn't mean living in the past.

Committing to healing doesn't mean dredging up old pain.

Committing to healing doesn't mean there's something wrong with you.

Committing to healing does mean noticing when you're stuck. It means being willing to explore whatever is interfering in any given moment until you find the hidden gem within the muck. It means freeing your energy to run clear again. Committing to healing is an act of courage and power on your own behalf.

In fact, the wounds you carry are a powerful source of the light you're here to shine in the world.

Again, I love Angeles Arrien's observation that "where we're challenged is where we're gifted." Isn't that great? This means our challenges are fertile with the seeds of our gifts. No matter how fierce the challenge, there is always some seed there that speaks to our gifts in the world.

Every challenge holds a seed of your authentic being and belonging.

Elise, the six-year-old daughter of a dear friend, once said: "Every seed has a promise. If you plant it and take care of it, it will grow and show you what it is."

How well are you tending the seeds of your becoming? Are they growing and showing you what they are — who you really are?

Now, not everyone gets tapped for as deep a healing process as I've taken on. My path has been to take on healing as a spiritual practice, because it's part of who I am and why I'm here. From an early age, at least as early as that little eight-year-old sitting with her dying sister, this was the most natural inclination in the world for me. I longed to make a difference for her, reading to her about Spirit and the truth of her being as a precious child of God.

My sister's death and other dynamics in my family gave me plenty of material to work with, motivating me to learn everything I can about how healing really happens. Gratefully, I was also gifted with stellar guides for the exploration, experts who knew the territory and could help show me the way through. I've been able to experience healing in ways that not only free the gifts bound up in my childhood challenges, but also to learn the energetics of both the wounding and the healing processes.

The cumulative effect of the innate abilities I came in with, and all that I've learned along the way, has resulted in discovering powerful ways to reach others and help them heal at deeper levels than they otherwise might have. And I believe you have something equally powerful inside you. I want you to know it's possible to free it up so you can live the life you dream of and make the difference *you* want to make.

People who know me well know that I frequently refer to "diving in" or going "deep." That's because there's lots of fertility in the depths. Think of the rich, fertile soil of the midwest heartland in the U.S., up to twenty feet deep in some places! That kind of fertility is inside us, too, where the seeds of our becoming lie in wait for the right conditions to spring into life. That's why we go deep, to give those seeds what they need for germination — so they can blossom fully!

Diving into that fertile ground brings the light needed for germination.

I hope you're beginning to appreciate the mighty act of power it took for you to hide yourself as completely as you did. It ought to be awe-inspiring! Can you imagine the sheer force of will you were capable of mustering?

So one of the reasons to dive deep is to release the power that's still bound up in trying to protect the seed of you — making sure you don't say the wrong thing, or do something that offends people, or reveal something of yourself you'd rather keep hidden.

Until now.

Can you imagine that power being freed up to serve other purposes — like working toward the realization of your life dreams?

Not that freedom comes in an instant. Healing does seem to be a lifelong endeavor, each dive and re-emergence bringing with it another joy.

In fact, while writing this book another layer (or two or three) of fear and panic took me by surprise when I realized that in order to write a book that might really make a difference, I was going to have to tell my own story.

I didn't get to hide behind the old, familiar professional facade.

For awhile, I felt terribly exposed, like someone tore back the cloak I'd so cleverly wrapped up in, exposing me for the fraud some part of me was sure I must be. I totally wanted to run back into hiding.

I could have run away from writing, but I actually wanted to face the fiercely challenging material that came up inside me. (That may sound a bit strange, but I've actually come to trust the journey in, down, through, and back out again. Like diving for jewels on the ocean floor!)

So, I dove in.

If you've been hiding and want to let the world see who you really are, find a healer you trust and start diving in.

Just a word about finding a good healer. There are a lot of great healing modalities out there, each of them with something beneficial to offer. I've tried most of them.

I can't know what is best for you, but generally speaking, in my experience, if you really want to make the difference *you* are here to make, then you'll want to find a healer who supports you to feel what you really feel and to dive deep when that's what's called for. Find someone who has a good grasp on both the energetic and psychological aspects of the healing process.

You'll want to work with someone who can meet and acknowledge you as you are and help you grow from there. Don't hesitate to schedule an initial consultation, ask questions, and find someone who really feels like a good fit. And let me be clear: while I'm clearly an advocate for doing deep healing work, you must be responsible for finding what works best for you.

In my experience, the more cognitive and behavioral (or medical) approaches to well-being won't get people like us all the way to where we want to go. They may be useful and important at times, but ultimately a more deeply transformative approach is required to clear the source of the challenges we face.

If you come across a deep cave in the earth and you want to know what's in there, you've got to get into the cave. If you want to experience all the splendor of the stalagmites and stalactites and the possibility of finding crystals, you've got to do more than get yourself to the entrance for a look in. You're going to have to pass through the entrance and begin the descent. You need a headlamp, but there are going to be places where even a headlamp won't show you what you're headed into, where all you can do is feel your way along one inch at a time.

And there are going to be some tight squeezes. This is where it's important to have support and guidance from somebody who's been there and can teach you how to breathe and maneuver your way through.

The rewards of going in and going down and coming through are worth every tear shed.

I want to share a story with you here. There are several versions of it, but here's how I remember it:

A number of years ago, a Buddhist monastery in Thailand was preparing for a big move to a new location. At the monastery was a huge clay statue of Buddha, so big it required a crane to move it. As the forks of the crane were inserted below the base of the Buddha, and they began to lift, someone noticed a crack forming in the clay. And it began to rain.

Concerned for the integrity of the Buddha, the head monk decided to postpone the move and throw a tarp over the statue. Later that night, he went out to check on the Buddha. As the light of the flashlight passed over the crack in the clay, he noticed something gleaming back at him. Something bright and sparkling. He gathered a few other monks and together they investigated further, slowly chiseling the clay away. When they were finished, there before them was a Buddha made of solid gold.

Apparently, centuries earlier there had been a war and invaders were headed toward the region of the monastery. The monks at the monastery at that time knew they needed to flee, but also knew they couldn't take the big, gold Buddha with them. So they covered it with clay. To protect it. Over time, the secret was lost and everyone came to assume the Buddha was indeed made of clay.

You get the point, right?

This is what we do as kids. We pile on layers of "clay" to protect our bright, shiny selves from people who can't see who we really are, from a world that wittingly or unwittingly inflicts hurt and pain. By the time we reach adulthood, we ourselves may have largely forgotten our golden light.

Our pure, innocent selves remain covered under layers of well-intended protective armoring, designed to maintain whatever sense of belonging we may have forged along the way, even if it means playing small or hiding our real feelings. Of course you had to hide!

Until you can't.

At a certain point, the clay starts to crack on its own. My guess is, if you're reading this, it has already started to crack and you may have already been doing some healing work.

You know that now's the time to start looking at what's really underneath all those layers!

Of course, unlike freeing the golden Buddha, we don't simply take an afternoon to chip away all the layers. We work more slowly, seeing something glimmering beneath the clay and getting curious about what's under there, then patiently releasing and revealing the true self. It's an immensely loving act, taken over and over again with each opening.

As each layer of armoring is released, the channels are restored for your pure life force to flow through. A wonderful sense of expansion comes in. The love in your heart flows more freely.

When you're not defending yourself from the outside world, you get to experience whatever comes your way, including all the good, true and beautiful in the world! Over time, that state of expansion becomes more the norm. In that state, you can't help but remember who you are and why you're here!

Yes, the process is fierce at times.

But Pachamama, mother earth (who's known in the Andes as "our one true mother") looks out for us. Spirit, God, the angels, ancestors, guides by whatever name, are looking out for you. They always have your best interests at heart. They've been protecting you, guiding you along the way until the right door opens at the right time for you to finally do whatever it takes to go retrieve all the power that's been tied up in self-protection, so you can put it to better use.

I hope you'll take that to heart. Let's be compassionate with ourselves, as well as courageous, as we work our way to the core of our true promise and potential.

Because isn't it all about love? Loving ourselves. Discovering just how lovable we really are and flowing the love in our own hearts out into the world in ways that bless others and make the world a better place.

And remember, because we're doubly challenged — in terms of childhood wounding and in terms of our disconnect from the land — we're also doubly blessed! As we heal, we're also poised to reclaim deeper connection to the land, which is the focus of the next chapter. These two complementary processes of healing and "landing" go hand in hand, leading us right into the immensely loving lap of Pachamama, our one true mother.

Dear Seeker,

What do you know about the seeds of your own magic? Where are you challenged? What do you still yearn to bring forth from within you?

Can you let your longing be a catalyst for discovery and a guide for finding the magic only you can give to the world? Are you ready to uncover more of who you are, why you're here, and how you belong?

I hope that if your longing is great enough you'll do whatever it takes to free yourself. I hope you'll find the support you need (if you don't already have it) to follow the catalytic call of your longing and that you'll engage a deep healing process whenever necessary.

I hope you'll tend the seed of you well so you can blossom and show the world who you really are.

Here's to clearing the channel for your love and light to flow through.

Blessings,

Kimberlie

CHAPTER FIVE

Original Wholeness

"She had a hundred precocious ideas, and some were good and true, but they could never be hers until she found them alone, for ideas are but words unless they are sown in experience."

WADE DAVIS, THE SERPENT AND THE RAINBOW

"Pachamama, your one true mother."

These words were first spoken into my awareness fourteen years ago.

The room is lit by candles, a faint scent of Agua de Florida hangs in the air, and the sound of rattles is persistent, intent on gathering the spirits to support this circle of newbie shamans receiving their first rites along the path of initiation.

Marti makes the rounds, visiting each one of us as we sit cross-legged on the floor. She is no longer simply Marti, our teacher and mentor. Entire lineages fill her being — each of the lineages into which she is initiated. She is Paqo, Shaman.

When she reaches me, I hear the same words she has spoken to each initiate in turn, but now they're for me. They're alive. They enter me and I feel their truth, especially these five words: "Pachamama, your one true mother."

The energy of those words stays with me, forming a seed inside, offering just a flash of their germination and blossoming in my life years later as The Wholeness Project, and then the vision folds itself up inside the seed again.

Oh, the love! A massive wave of joy washes over me as Marti moves on to the next person in the circle.

Fourteen years ago, I had no idea what lay ahead for me in terms of the unfolding of that seed through my work. I certainly had no idea of the depths to which I would dive to retrieve my own soul, and I had no idea how profoundly I would come to know Pachamama as my one true mother.

As you continue reading, I hope you'll also feel Pachamama's great love for you. I want to begin showing you how you, too, can reclaim wholeness by tapping into the land right where you are and the land where you were born. Although this wisdom has always been here, we're so disconnected from it that we don't often even think to look for it.

Some of what I'll be describing to you may sound a bit radical — and it is. But as the wisdom-keepers of the world have always known, this knowledge is fundamental to the well-being of Pachamama and all her children.

As I share some of what I've learned about wholeness, you can begin finding your origins in the land, too, especially the landscapes of your birth that inform who you are and what you came to do. You'll begin sensing a bigger belonging — to know that in addition to your human communities, you belong to a region of collective consciousness that's expressed in the land where you live and where you were born. It's a connection that will help you be more mindfully present, to see and be seen more clearly, to love and be loved more fully. It's a connection that creates wholeness — original, indigenous wholeness.

These two words, original and indigenous, can be used interchangeably. They both speak to our origins in the land. The word indigenous has its roots in the Latin word "*indigena*," "sprung from the land." The word "original" also sources from Latin, "*originem*" meaning "beginning, source, birth" and "*oriri*," meaning "to rise" (according to the Online Etymology Dictionary).

Both words speak to a connection with earth that is innate and natural. It's a connection Western culture has largely lost, and, I believe, must be reclaimed! And once reclaimed, the connection again becomes inarguable and sacred. It becomes the source — of grounding, of belonging, of our unique and individual presence in the greater whole.

We tend to think of wholeness as a longed-for destination we set our sights on and toward which we journey to finally, hopefully one day arrive — no missing parts, complete, intact, and content.

But what if wholeness is more a way to engage the journey, rather than the destination itself — more verb than noun?

In the modern world, we have a pervasive sense that something important is missing.

We've become distracted from the source of true wholeness.

Oh, how we yearn for some imagined arrival where our needs are met, our dreams come true, and we can finally be at peace! We're driven to find a magical something out there that will complete us, make us happy, and bring us whole.

But we look in all the wrong places. The yearning sets us off on what can be an endless journey of searching for the right job, the perfect partner, enough money, the ideal teacher.... Occasionally we think we've found "it," and then, when the magic wears off, we take up the search again.

If you take a moment to tap into your own sense of something missing, your own longing, do you find the imagined solution is always future-based? It'll come when you graduate, when you get your business going, when you meet the perfect partner, after the kids leave home, once you get through menopause. You'll find it when you're "ready" (and clearly you're not ready yet!). Why does it seem to be always out of reach?

But here's the deal: It is entirely possible to find that missing something right where you are, and in a way that will bring you ever more alive and more engaged in the adventure of life. It's right here, right now, always with you, always available.

The thing that's missing is our relationship with the land.

There is a way of being awake, aware, and in relationship with the land as a conscious, living being — with Pachamama — that meets our yearning. This relationship completes us. It plugs us into existence in a way that begins to answer those core questions we carry: Who am I? Why am I here? Where do I belong?

Spirit speaks us into being through the land. And the land speaks us whole.

Imagine this: Earth and all of nature form a great web of life — an actual world wide web, brought into being by Great Spirit, God, the Creator — whatever name works for you. It's a beautiful weaving of life in which every element is an important aspect of the whole. And you're a vital part of it, too — each of us is, no matter how invisible, alone, or separate we might at times sense ourselves to be.

Our connection to the web brings wholeness. Indigenous people living where they were born, in close ongoing relationship with the land, have always known this. They haven't lost their profound connection with all that is. Their home is the whole of earth and sky — the palpable experience of belonging to rivers, mountains, lakes, valleys and plains, with sun and moon and stars above.

As I've explored Andean wisdom, I've learned that "wholeness" is a primary organizing principle of consciousness through which humans can create lives that flourish. Organized by wholeness, we tap into the source of creative action. We live on the growing edge of our becoming, generate creative ways to germinate and grow our seeds, and create momentum as we go.

I'm now passionate about sharing this understanding of wholeness because I believe it's key to our capacity for making a genuine and lasting difference in the world.

Where do we start? By bringing presence and awareness to the land right where we are.

After decades spent disconnected from earth and body — my initial attempts to restore wholeness were in some ways quite simple and in other ways fierce.

First, I learned to fill myself with the energies of earth, sunlight, and air, which takes just a few minutes every day. You can do this, too:

Stand on earth and breathe earth energy up into your body, then exhale to disperse it where it's needed in your body. Seven breaths. Then seven breaths to bring sunlight into and through your body. And then feed your heart with the spaciousness of air itself, again with seven breaths. It's a great practice to start your day with, and easy to do anytime you need to rejuvenate your energy.

Another, more challenging practice, is one that Angeles Arrien suggests to her students: to spend an hour outside in nature every day for a year, without missing a single day.

I took this on early in my training and initiation. It was fierce, but I did it.

No matter how cold (think January in Colorado) or hot (okay, now think July in Colorado), whether I had a flight to catch that day or was fighting off a cold, I was out there, doing my best to be aware of what was happening in the natural world.

My fear around showing up authentically began to recede. I began to see more of my true nature reflected back to me from nature. I began to relax, knowing I was finally headed home.

If you take on this practice, I'd love to hear what you discover.

But there's more. To restore wholeness in our transient culture, we need a root system that reaches wide — *one that includes our birthplace*. One that reconnects us to our original point of emergence on the planet, the place where we were born. This may sound like a strange thing, but once people experience it, they say it makes a lot of sense.

To give you more of a sense of how your birthplace holds secrets to who you are and why you're here, I'll share with you some of what my birthplace has revealed since I began taking a closer look a few years ago. I know it's a radical idea, but there really is magic for you in the land where you were born!

(These discoveries stem from Marti Spiegelman's charge to her students to "become the powers of the geographies where you were born.")

I was born in Great Falls, Montana, on the plains east of the Rocky Mountains. When we moved to western Montana, I was just two months old. I didn't return to Great Falls again until I was 50 years old.

Just a few years into my initiation at that point, Marti encouraged me to return to the land of my birth to make an offering to the Missouri River, the longest river in North America, that flows right through the city and beside which I was born.

Arriving on a Thursday afternoon in October, I made the offering the next morning in freezing temperatures, and left town again by noon. I was in no way impressed by the city or the land, and certainly didn't take the time to get to know it better.

A couple of years later, I realized something that should have been obvious all along. I was born in Great *Falls*. There was a waterfall there!

Correction — not just one waterfall, but five of them, one right after another through and just beyond the city, which I think is just totally amazing.

According to Andean perception, waterfalls are places of emergence between the worlds, where new ideas are born and take life in this world. When I teach, whether it's one on one or in a group, I source the energy of waterfalls to help people bring pieces of their genius forward from the unseen world into this world.

So, excited by this discovery, I planned another road trip to Great Falls.

This time, I took note of the landscape all along the way, taking in the energies as I drove — of the river, a long and beautiful canyon, the prairie, and an occasional butte overlook. The land came alive, revealing how Great Falls fits into the larger landscape.

Once in the city, I visited two of the falls — Black Eagle (the only one actually in town) and Colter. Four of the falls have been dammed, with the remaining one submerged behind another. At Black Eagle, I made some offerings, with thanks and prayers and a promise to embody those sacred energies in my life.

Later, headed north toward Glacier Park, the prairie also came alive. Sweetgrass. A beautiful, vast ocean of golden sweetgrass swaying in the wind, filled the air with its sweetness, catching the sun just so. So this is me, too, I thought. This soft, easy way of being on earth. But more than that, I also saw the roots.

The magic is in the roots. The massive, deep root systems of the prairie hold the land in place.

Inwardly, I celebrated this beautiful expression of another piece of my own purpose: To help people reconnect with their own roots — to hold their inner land in place so their true natures can rise and shine in the sun.

I was already teaching my clients about this radical way of grounding in the land of their birthplaces, but I didn't see the roots of that work in my own roots until, well, until I did. Talk about confirmation! When I finally saw the prairie for what it really is, for the enormous role it plays in holding earth in place, it was one of those "gently hit the side of your head while saying *duuhhh*" moments!

I've seen my clients have those moments, too. Like the yoga teacher whose eyes reveal deep pools of wisdom, but who initially feared the huge lake on whose shores she was born. Back turned toward it, she preferred looking the other direction, out to the hills. Then one day, the lake tapped her on the shoulder and when she looked back, she saw her own reflection in the water. Eventually she dived in, and her access to the depth of all that wisdom has grown immensely since then. Her business is growing. And of course her own students (as well as the community she lives in) are benefitting from the new depth in her teaching.

Or the wilderness guide whose change in lifestyle left her feeling lost, adrift. She, too, was born in prairie land created when an ancient ocean receded and left behind the deep fertile soil out of which prairie grasses grow. She'd resonated with that sense of blowing in the wind like the grasses, her energy body floating high as she remained unaware of and unable to tap her deeper wisdom.

Then she found the deep ancient soils. Or they found her. (It's always inspiring to watch a reconnection, the recognition and snapping together that happens between place and human, human and place.) What I know is that the shift in her was instant. Her energy body came back down around her, the fear in her eyes subsided, and her faith that she can and will bring forth her own gifts became unshakeable. A short time later she remembered her passion for writing and returned to a project she'd abandoned years ago — a project that's sure to inspire her readers to a bigger life.

One more example. An entrepreneur, about to launch her own coaching program, vacillated between hiding behind work that was familiar to her but not her real passion — and dreaming big into the difference she knows she can make in others' lives. She was born in the Midwest near ancient burial mounds and caves — places where it's easy to go inside and hide. Then she discovered some hills. She could stand on them and be really visible, which made her feel super vulnerable until she discovered they were aligned with the complementary energies of caves and springs. Rather than vacillate between above and below, visibility and invisibility, she can now inhabit the whole landscape, with access to the wisdom in each of those landforms. She's growing in leaps and bounds, shaping the work she will soon launch in ways that are going to make a huge difference for young people.

My own root system now runs far and wide around the planet, connected to power places that feed my imagination and inform my work as mentor and teacher.

You can create roots like this, too. And then use them. Wherever you are — even inside your home or flying on an airplane, you can access the power of the land.

Try this: Travel back in time and space to your own birth. Where did you make your appearance on the planet? Take a moment to envision that land. Can you see the surrounding landscape? Not the buildings and all the manmade stuff, but the land itself.

Are there mountains? Rivers? Desert, plains, hills, a peninsula? Lakes?

Sense the weaving of the surrounding landscape.

There's a specific place in the weaving where Spirit said, "This dear one — I want her to pop through right here. Here, in this landscape. Her magic is of these hills and creeks, these forested lakes, this alluvial fan formed eons ago (or whatever the landscape around you reveals). She is of the powers of this land, and they will show her who she is. They will help to reveal her purpose on the planet."

Even if you've been transplanted, your original root system is still in that land.

And you can set your intention right now to sense your root system once again intact. Right where you are in this moment, imagine you have roots that run all the way to your birthplace and the surrounding geographies.

People consistently report experiencing a greater sense of presence, confidence, and belonging when they practice this.

To reconnect with your indigenous wholeness in the land right where you are and through which you were originally spoken into being — and to let that connection take up resonance in your bones — is to optimize the conditions for the chunk of wisdom encoded in your DNA to unfold optimally. To know where you come from is to know the seed of you, your roots, and the conditions needed for your germination and blossoming.

Tapping into the land that speaks you whole, you'll grow ever stronger, ever more beautifully and visibly into the world. This is what it means to come alive in full presence, so connected to the source of your light that you never again have to question your place in the world!

....

Dear Seeker,

Know this: You are dearly loved.

Where you've been hiding out, feeling shy or unsupported, Pachamama calls you to her lap with the promise of love and of acknowledgement for your true gifts.

That which you long for is longing for you, and loving you and gesturing wildly toward your belonging, your passion, and your purpose!

You are *a seed, a sacred potential spoken into being by Spirit through the land. Right where you are, Pachamama is streaming you into being, with her undying love and acceptance, as valued and precious as all of her children. The connection is there to be made.*

Say yes!

In wholeness,

Kimberlie

GROWING FORWARD

I want to extend to you my big thanks for following my ongoing journey to wholeness. I hope some previously unrecognized seeds of possibility are waking up in you, sparked into life by the message of this book.

The message is, of course, far beyond me or any one of us individually. Its source and reach are universal. To align yourself with an original, indigenous experience of wholeness is to heal, to get clear about who you are, and weave your being into the greater tapestry of life.

And if life has taught me anything it is that mentoring is vital for true wholeness. Those questions we all carry — "Who am I?" "Why am I here?" "Where do I belong?" — can only be answered as we discover how intimately connected we are to each other, to nature, to Spirit's great design for the planet we call home. We're poised for a grand new adventure here on planet earth, one that requires tapping into a mostly forgotten knowledge of wholeness now beginning to come back into collective awareness.

If you are called to join the growing movement of people like you who value the power of mentoring and who want to bring their gifts to light through the power of original, transformative wholeness, your next step is to schedule a complimentary initial consultation with me at www.kimberlie.acuityscheduling.com.

If you simply want some beginning practices to start exploring on your own, your next step is to download my free PDF gift to you — Feet on the Ground Healing and Wholeness: Practices for Discovering your True Nature. *You'll find it at* www.thewholenessproject.com.

As they say to give thanks in the Andes... Sulpayqi! I genuinely hope we'll get to connect again along the way.

Here's to waking up... in wholeness.

ACKNOWLEDGEMENTS

It takes a village, and without these beloved individuals my book would never have come to be. How grateful I am for the presence of each and every one of you in my life.

Kate Makled, my editor. I had no idea what an editor *really* does until I took on this project, and you've set the bar high! You had a knack for asking the right question at the right time so I could walk into this book whole. Thank you.

Angela Lauria, my publisher. Wow. Just wow. Such a force of love you are! I see your passion for making a difference in the world transforming lives with every book you publish, and I'm thrilled that you're publishing mine. Your brilliance is undeniable, and I thank you for championing my fierce rite of passage into published author.

Marti Spiegelman, masterful mentor and teacher whose heart is as big as the sea. You've gifted me an authentic initiation, a global ayllu, inspiration to dream big, and powerful technologies of consciousness with which to create my life in wholeness. Diospagarasunki.

Don Manuel Quispe, spiritual leader of the Andean nation of Q'eros, primary teacher of wholeness, and teacher of my teacher. I honor your spirit and wisdom, now guiding us from another realm.

Peter Tsantilis, healer, mentor and transformative witness. You've blessed my life immeasurably.

Ellen Bachmeyer, my initiatory sister and ally, a great visionary. Your generous presence was quite literally always available whether I wanted to run a passage by you, process a challenge, or celebrate a victory. What a great gift to walk this awe-inspiring journey of discovery with you.

Peggy Utesch, my spirit sister and beautiful friend for life. Thank you for being a co-conspirator in magic-making each time we meet... and for perfect edits when I needed them most!

To my clients and students, I'm in awe as I behold the seeds of your genius germinate and blossom in wholeness before my very eyes.

For my parents and sisters, and all the familial forces that have helped shape the course of my amazing life — in grief and in joy — I am deeply grateful. I love you all.

My husband, Jim, who compassionately witnessed many a wakeful night, whether the muses were working overtime or my anxiety closet had flung wide open. While I simply must thank you for your magical gift for spot-on editorial feedback, I'm most deeply grateful for your radical acceptance when you found yourself suddenly widowed for the summer as this book was born — it means the world to me! "Together, we always secret a how."

And finally, Shams, rainbow warrior of a dog who adopted us forever ago and spent hours curled up under the desk as I wrote. I know you're close to crossing the rainbow bridge, and I'm grateful for your presence throughout this birth.

ABOUT THE AUTHOR

Kimberlie Chenoweth, author, mentor, and founder of *The Wholeness Project*™ is a natural at getting to the core of things — your uniqueness, your potential, and whatever gets in the way of being all you can be. She loves helping gifted healers, artists, teachers, and visionaries reclaim wholeness — to reconnect to the source of their abilities so they can get their good work out into the world the way it's intended to be.

A bit of a mystic by nature, Kimberlie has studied visionary traditions of the East, West, and native Americas. She has sat in silence, traveled widely, and committed to a process of deep healing and transformation over many years. She is an Andean mesa carrier with a cross-cultural initiation. Through Shaman's Light™ training program and teachers in the Andes, Nepal, Tibet, and Ireland, Kimberlie has received out of the ordinary knowledge and tools for transformation that she's passionate about sharing with others.

Kimberlie has a Master's degree in Counseling. She's a certified Master NLP Practitioner and an endorsed member of the Core Transformation Trainers Association. After 20 years in private practice as a psychotherapist and personal development trainer, she launched The Wholeness Project™ in 2012.

Kimberlie lives in rural Western Colorado with her husband, two dogs, beautiful sunsets, and access to tantalizing hiking trails. She rarely leaves the house without her camera.

www.thewholenessproject.com

ABOUT DIFFERENCE PRESS

difference press

Difference Press offers entrepreneurs, including life coaches, healers, consultants, and community leaders, a comprehensive solution to get their books written, published, and promoted. A boutique-style alternative to self-publishing, Difference Press boasts a fair and easy-to-understand profit structure, low-priced author copies, and author-friendly contract terms. Its founder, Dr. Angela Lauria, has been bringing to life the literary ventures of hundreds of authors-in-transformation since 1994.

LET'S MAKE A DIFFERENCE WITH YOUR BOOK

You've seen other people make a difference with a book. Now it's your turn. If you are ready to stop watching and start taking massive action, reach out.

"Yes, I'm ready!"

In a market where hundreds of thousands books are published every year and are never heard from again, all participants of The Author Incubator have bestsellers that are actively changing lives and making a difference.

In two years we've created over 134 bestselling books in a row, 90% from first-time authors. We do this by selecting the highest quality and highest potential applicants for our future programs.

Our program doesn't just teach you how to write a book—our team of coaches, developmental editors, copy editors, art directors, and marketing experts incubate you from book idea to published bestseller, ensuring that the book you create can actually make a difference in the world. Then we give you the training you need to use your book to make the difference you want to make in the world, or to create a business out of serving your readers. If you have life-or world-changing ideas or services, a servant's heart, and the willingness to do what it REALLY takes to make a difference in the world with your book, go to http://theauthorincubator.com/apply/ to complete an application for the program today.

OTHER BOOKS BY DIFFERENCE PRESS

Clarity Alchemy: When Success Is Your Only Option

by Ann Bolender

Cracking the Code: A Practical Guide to Getting You Hired

by Molly Mapes

Divorce to Divine: Becoming the Fabulous Person You Were Intended to Be

by Cynthia Claire

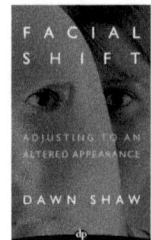

Facial Shift: Adjusting to an Altered Appearance

by Dawn Shaw

Finding Clarity: Design a Business You Love and Simplify Your Marketing

by Amanda H. Young

Flourish: Have It All Without Losing Yourself

by Dr. Rachel Talton

Marketing To Serve: The Entrepreneur's Guide to Marketing to Your Ideal Client and Making Money with Heart and Authenticity

by Cassie Parks

NEXT: How to Start a Successful Business That's Right for You and Your Family

by Caroline Greene

Pain Free: How I Released 43 Years of Chronic Pain

by Dottie DuParcé (Author), John F. Barnes (Foreword)

Secret Bad Girl: A Sexual Trauma Memoir and Resolution Guide

by Rachael Maddox

Skinny: The Teen Girl's Guide to Making Choices, Getting the Thin Body You Want, and Having the Confidence You've Always Dreamed Of

by Melissa Nations

The Aging Boomers: Answers to Critical Questions for You, Your Parents and Loved Ones

by Frank M. Samson

The Incubated Author: 10 Steps to Start a Movement with Your Message

by Angela Lauria

The Intentional Entrepreneur: How to Be a Noisebreaker, Not a Noisemaker

by Jen Dalton (Author), Jeanine Warisse Turner (Foreword)

The Paws Principle: Front Desk Conversion Secrets for the Vet Industry

by Scott Baker

Turn the Tide: Rise Above Toxic, Difficult Situations in the Workplace

by Kathy Obear

www.ingramcontent.com/pod-product-compliance
Lightning Source LLC
LaVergne TN
LVHW020935090426
835512LV00020B/3374